The TEDDY BEAR STORY

Josa Keyes

MMB

Contents

Teddy Bears At Large   6

Literary Bears   18

Some Famous Bears
    And Their People   32

Collecting Bears   44

Handmade Bears   66

Teddies And Children   76

Some teddy bears from the author's collection: *left to right*, Cherry, Fosters (a valuable, pre-First World War teddy found in an old cottage), Ted (the most usual teddy bear name) and Edward.

Teddy Bears At Large

The fact that you have picked up this book means that you are, very probably, an arctophile. There's no need to look alarmed, however – you share this distinction with literally millions of other perfectly sane people of all ages. An arctophile is simply someone who loves bears. The word is taken from the Greek "arktos", meaning bear, and "philos", meaning friend. Arctophiles everywhere agree that there is nothing like a teddy bear for constant and unswerving companionship, comfort, and dependability. They have been called the world's most popular stuffed toys, tops among countless other species. Why? Probably because real bears have such endearingly human qualities – they stand upright and can hug with their front paws, without being as disturbingly close to us as monkeys or apes.

Theodore Roosevelt, who gave his name to the teddy bear, was very keen on real bears. He hunted them, but he also enjoyed watching them going about their business. He explained the attraction in his book *Outdoor Pastimes of an American Hunter*, published in 1905: "On one occasion the bear was hard at work digging up squirrel or gopher caches on the side of a pine-clad hill; while at this work he looked rather like a large badger . . . it was extremely interesting to note the grotesque, half-human movements, and giant awkward strength of the great beast. He would twist the carcass around with the utmost ease, sometimes taking it in his forepaws and half-lifting, half shoving it. Once the bear lost his grip and rolled over during the course of some movement, and this made him angry, and he struck the carcass a savage whack, just as a pettish child will strike a table against which it has knocked itself . . ."

Wherever real bears are found, they inspire respect. Bears, of course, are not to be treated lightly, being so fierce and strong. The Indians knew all about them. Some tribes considered them so sacred that they never hunted them. Other tribes did, but always made sure that the dead animal's bones were arranged in the right order, so that he would not reach the Happy Hunting Ground crippled.

Russia is of course swarming with bears: the most common bear's name in their folklore tales is Mishka. Russian children have been playing with Mishka bears for centuries. In recent years, however, he has been successfully challenged by Vinni-Pukh, or the British Winnie the Pooh, who has taken his place alongside Mishka in Russian children's hearts. This did not prevent Mishka from being the mascot for the 1980 Olympic Games held in Moscow. There were choruses of dancing Mishkas in the opening celebrations, plus Mishka balloons and soft toys: he is a dear little thing, squatting on his haunches and smiling enthusiastically.

Now we come to a problem: the birth of Bruno Edwardus, or The Teddy Bear Himself, is wrapped in an impenetrable cloud of confusion and mystery. There are two claimants to the high honor of being his parent, and two large and successful companies have been based on his success. It is impossible to tell who was first, however, so you must judge for yourself from the evidence put before you. Personally, I think that it really does not matter who made the first teddy bear, in 1902, or why they did it: what is really important is the amount of happiness these silent little companions have given countless numbers of people ever since.

The American claim is based on Clifford Berryman's famous cartoon "Drawing the Line in Mississippi". This showed President Theodore Roosevelt refusing to shoot an appealing little bear held on a rope by a fierce-looking man in a hat. It referred to the President's settling of a border dispute between Louisiana and Mississippi in November 1902; he literally drew the official line between the two states. Legend has it that

someone caught a bear cub and tied it to a tree for the President to shoot during one of his numerous hunting trips. Naturally he was a great sportsman and a humane man, who would surely have drawn the line at shooting a trapped little animal. A member of his family could not recall ever hearing of such an incident, and there is certainly no record of it. But the cartoon caused a sensation: Teddy Roosevelt had found the animal which was to remain with him as a "signature" for the rest of his life. Certainly he never again appeared in a Berryman cartoon without his furry little companion. The President may have been somewhat embarrassed by all the fuss, but the teddy bear was immensely valuable to him in endearing him to an animal-loving public.

Whatever happened, the seed had been sown. Morris Michtom, a Russian immigrant to America who had all the natural Russian affection for, and interest in, bears, saw the cartoon and was inspired. He and his wife owned a candy store in Brooklyn, New York, where they also sold home-made toys. The baby bear seemed an excellent idea for a new stuffed toy, with built-in publicity before it was even sewn together! Michtom obtained brown plush fabric to resemble as closely as possible a real bear's fur, and gave his creation moveable arms and legs and button eyes. Then he placed "Teddy's bear" in the candy store window with a copy of the cartoon. Naturally, someone fell in love with the bear at first sight, and he was bought almost immediately. The Michtoms hurried to replace him, and soon they were selling as many as they could make.

It is difficult to extricate the facts from the next part of the story, as the evidence has disappeared, but Michtom is said to have written to the President, enclosing a specially-made bear, asking respectfully if he could use the name "Teddy" for the new toy. A handwritten reply apparently arrived in due course, saying that Roosevelt could not see what earthly use his name might be in the toy bear business, but that Michtom was welcome to use it. Neither of these two letters now exists, which is a great pity, as undoubtedly the Presidential letter would have been a remarkable trophy. Framed and exhibited, it would have been wonderful publicity for the Michtom bear. Its reported tone does ring true in the light of the President's bewilderment at his connection with stuffed toys!

Michtom's Teddy Bears were such a success, with or without the letters, that he started his own company on the strength of them. Today it is known as the Ideal Toy Corporation, and is one of the biggest toy manufacturers in America. But he could not hang on to his brilliant idea for long, as trade names could not be given copyright in those days. Soon everyone was jumping on the teddy bear band wagon, and our furry friends were selling well in many American stores as early as 1904.

The story of the other contender for the "first teddy title" starts with a remarkable German lady named Margarete Steiff. She had been very ill with polio when a child, which left her wheelchair-bound and unable to walk. Instead of giving up, however, Margarete refused to be a burden to anyone, and decided to earn her own living. She possessed one of the earliest

Facing page, top Brown bear (Ursus arctos), widespread around the world, with a charming expression, and the strength to hug you to death.

Facing page, bottom Theodore Roosevelt (1858-1919), twenty-sixth president of the United States, skilled explorer, huntsman, and "father" of the teddy bear.

Left Bully Bear, Peter Bull's cartoon teddy bear, explores his origins in *Bully Bear Goes to Hollywood*, illustrated by Enid Irving.

Above The famous Clifford Berryman cartoon, which appeared in the Washington Evening Star on November 18, 1902.

hand-driven sewing machines, set up back to front so that she could wind the handle with her damaged left hand. She became a dressmaker, and managed to lead a full and independent life, surrounded by a loving family and many friends, young and old.

One day, Margarete happened to make herself a gray felt pin-cushion, in the shape of an elephant. Her younger friends fell on this "toy" with cries of delight: she didn't have a chance to stick pins in it. The elephants became very popular, so much so that she had to stop giving them away and begin to make them full-time, with the help of her sister and other local women. Soon she was producing 5,000 elephants a year, shortly to be joined by monkeys, donkeys, horses, pigs and camels. By 1893, she was really in business, and her range of animals sold well at the famous Leipzig fair that year.

At this point, Margarete decided to employ her two nephews, Richard and Paul Steiff, in the family business. To Richard must go the credit for making the first German bear. He had trained as an artist, and spent much time at the Stuttgart Zoological Gardens searching for inspiration for new stuffed toys. He particularly liked the bear pits, and from his sketches produced a toy bear with movable joints and a swivelling head. His aunt was not very happy with it at first. She thought the toy too big and heavy, and the mohair of which it was made was difficult to obtain in those days. After several experiments, however, a satisfactory model appeared with the "Knopf im

Ohr" (button in ear), which was to become characteristic of the Steiff bears. It was known as "Friend Petz".

The bears were exhibited, along with all Margarete's other toys, at the Leipzig fair in 1902 where they were seen by a buyer from F.A.O. Schwartz in America. This proved to be the turning point in their fortunes: the buyer put in a massive order, and the bears' names were changed to "Teddy" for the benefit of the American children who were to receive them.

Facing page A chorus of dancing Mishka bears at the opening celebrations of the 1982 Moscow Olympic Games. Mishka bear is a popular subject for Russian folk tales, and Russian children had toy Mishkas long before teddy bears arrived.

Left The crowd holds up different-colored cards to create a giant Mishka in the Moscow Olympic stadium. There were also inflatable Mishkas and soft toy Mishkas – the Russian version of a teddy.

Above An original early Steiff bear, sold at Sotheby's, London. Note his long arms, broad hips, big paws and plain button eyes.

There is a legend connecting the Steiff bears to President Roosevelt. The story goes that little Steiff bears, dressed as huntsmen to honor the father of the bride, were used to decorate the tables at the wedding reception of the President's daughter, Alice. An amused guest asked the President what species of bear they might be; another guest is said to have replied wittily for him: "Teddy Bears." This story has a fairytale charm, but alas was disproved by that indefatigable seeker after teddy truth, the late Peter Bull. He actually went to visit Alice Longworth, then over eighty, to ask what had really happened at her wedding reception. She stated her dislike of teddy bears and said that not only could she remember every detail of her wedding reception, but she had photographs to prove that there hadn't been a teddy bear in sight! The wedding took place in 1906, four years after the Berryman cartoon was first published.

In the Smithsonian Institute in Washington, there sits the "original teddy", which came from the Roosevelt home. Peter Bull didn't think he looked old enough to be the original one, and having seen him myself, I don't think he is either. But I also think it doesn't matter who he is. He can be the unknown teddy soldier, representing all brave teddy bears who have served faithfully in nurseries and homes all over the world.

So there is all the evidence: I hope you agree with me that it really doesn't matter who made the first teddy bear. Besides, a most unusual little black stuffed bear was sold at Sotheby's, London, recently for $430. His owner was over ninety, and had owned him since she was a small baby, proving that there were much-loved bears in existence long before all the fuss started in 1902. Moreover, with such a long tradition of Mishka bears in Russia, it seems unlikely that Russian children did not have stuffed Mishka toys, as well as wooden and tin ones.

The important thing about the teddy bear is that he provides people of all ages with something they need. It might be a feeling of continuity with their own past, a reminder of childhood, or for children, a tremendous focus for fantasy and play, affection, security and secrets.

Facing page A varied collection of teddy bears sold at Sotheby's, London, in 1984. The little dark bear on the top step belonged to an old lady of ninety, who had had him since she was a baby. He was made before 1902, and is a pre-teddy bear.

Top Children and their teddies getting ready for bed. The girl in the middle holds a Paddington toy bear.

Left An original Steiff teddy bear wearing an unoriginal boater and bow-tie, both of which helped push his price up to $950 when he was sold at Sotheby's, London. Steiff have recently created a fine gray plush reproduction of their earliest teddy bear.

13

Many children prefer teddies to dolls. This might be because most dolls are not so easily cuddled, and, although they are often beautiful, they lack the sympathetic expression of a teddy bear. A teddy's face improves with age and love; a battered doll, because she is more like a real person, tends to look rather sinister. (Which is not to say, of course, that dolls cannot be loved by their little owners even when they are in the most appalling condition!)

A really good, high quality teddy bear should last a long time. Cheaper teddies, although appealing to start with, tend not to last the course so well. My little teddy, sitting by my desk, dates from about 1910. He is balding rapidly, his squeaker no longer works, and someone has stitched his original hump down flat, but he is beautifully made and he has retained his dignity and appeal to this day.

Left Winnie the Pooh reaches for "a little something" to eat from the top shelf, in A. A. Milne's story *Piglet Meets a Heffalump*, illustrated by E. H. Shepard.

Above "Only YOU Can Prevent Forest Fires," says Smokey Bear, potent symbol of the Forest Service's successful anti-forest fire campaign. Ideal Toys' stuffed Smokey came with an application to become a Junior Forest Ranger, encouraging childrens' awareness of forest fire-prevention.

Above European teddy bear postcards from Rose Wharnsby's huge collection. Her teddy bear, Poohscard, runs a Junior Postcard Club in Britain.

Albert the Butcher from the International Teddy Bear Club's 1984 calendar: "All the choicest cuts for his customers with a cheery smile and a constant flow of merriment. He could raise a smile on even the most grim faced person . . ."

Chapter 2

Winnie the Pooh is presented with a Special Pencil Case for rescuing Piglet from the flood. He is surrounded by Rabbit, Kanga, Piglet, Roo and Owl, all making helpful remarks like, "Open it, Pooh", "I know what it is", and "No, you don't".

Literary Bears

If you love teddy bears, you have probably dipped into some of the many books written about them. Bears in literature are nearly always a force for positive good. The real bear's fierce nature is almost entirely banished in a teddy's loving gentleness. The one constant bear characteristic however, is his well-known greediness, especially for honey! Winnie the Pooh is very fond of his "little something", usually at 11 o'clock. The Roosevelt Bears will eat anything, astonishing their human audience by the amount and variety of food consumed. Paddington is firmly addicted to marmalade (and his creator, Michael Bond, is very fond of it too). Peter Bull's Bully Bear has a more exotic taste: peanut butter.

The best authors have created unique characters for their furry heroes. Teddy might be full of stuffing, but he knows what is right and always holds onto his moral sense, even when there is dreadful (usually edible) temptation. Paddington is full of sharp looks for wrongdoers, and takes immediate, if somewhat chaotic, action. The Roosevelt bears are keen to help unfortunate children with their robbers' gold. Pooh, although he is not meant to have much in the way of a brain, is very brave and kind, and nobly rescues Piglet from the flood.

There were of course many literary bears before 1902 – think of Goldilocks, cheekily trespassing into porridge and beds – but teddy himself was given a tremendous boost by the popular newspaper serial *The Roosevelt Bears*, written by Seymour Eaton (Paul Piper). These characters do admittedly look like real bears, but it is obvious they were inspired by the growing craze for teddies. Their rhyming adventures started in 1905:

"*Two Roosevelt Bears have a home out West*
In a big ravine near a mountain crest . . ."

The first book, *The Roosevelt Bears – Their Travels and Adventures*, has just been re-published by Dover Publications. It describes what happened when the genial pair left their mountain home by train to travel around America seeing the sights, and meeting the children. Seymour Eaton describes his work as "a good, wholesome yarn, arranged in a merry jingle." He felt himself to be quite justified in using the name

Above The Traveling Bears in New York, by Seymour Eaton (Paul Piper), illustrated by R. K. Culver following the style created by Floyd Campbell. The Roosevelt Bears visit the sights in New York, and on the way back they meet their namesake.

"Roosevelt" in the title, and cashing in on the teddy bear craze, as "the President and his boys have been pleased with the story as it appeared in serial form."

Eaton apparently based some of the bears' mischief on the misdemeanors of children he knew, but there is a strong tone of education and admonition mixed in with the pranks:

"*A speech was made by Teddy-B*
Who told the boys and girls that he
Believed in fun and honest strife,
And manly sport and strenuous life . . ."

Unfortunately, this doesn't stop the bears from scribbling graffiti on the Bunker Hill monument, or from being put in prison for an automobile offense.

The first volume was illustrated by V. Floyd Campbell, who made them look very real and bear-like, but with the most expressive faces. The bears usually sported large smiles (especially when confronted with a huge slice of chocolate cake). Campbell even managed to make them look very comfortable in clothes, while still retaining their natural bear-ness. The books' popularity declined after the First World

War, when children began to demand prose stories, but they do have undoubted old-world charm. The first volume was followed by three more, the last being *The Bear Detectives*, which had the bears solving nursery mysteries, such as the whereabouts of Bo Peep's sheep's tails. All four volumes are much sought after by collectors today, as are the framed color pictures, chinaware and jugs which depicted the bears. At the time, however, the books were banned from some libraries, as they were thought to be badly written.

Many children's stories have been written about teddy bears, but surely none have captured the world's imagination as much as the adventures of Winnie the Pooh. It all started in 1920, when Daphne Milne bought a teddy bear in Harrods, London, for her little son's first birthday. Her husband was A.A. Milne, who wrote at the time for the humorous magazine, *Punch*. Their little boy, Christopher Robin, became very attached to his birthday bear, and named him Winnie, after a favorite bear

Above President Theodore Roosevelt, his wife Edith, and their children, left to right, Quentin (5), Ted (15), Archie (9), Alice (19), Kermit (13) and Ethel (11).

in the London Zoo, and Pooh, after a swan he used to feed.

A.A. Milne was inspired to write the stories by hearing Christopher Robin putting on a "growly voice", and speaking for his teddy bear. There are twenty stories in all, divided into two books: *Winnie the Pooh*, and *The House at Pooh Corner*, and they appeal strongly to children and adults alike. Both books are dedicated to Daphne, making clear the important role she played in their genesis:

"You gave me Christopher Robin, and then
You breathed new life in Pooh,
Whatever of each has left my pen
Goes homing back to you.
My book is ready, and comes to greet
The mother it longs to see –
It would be my present to you, my sweet,
If it weren't your gift to me."

The stories apparently emerged from a family game, which involved both devoted parents, their little boy, and all his stuffed animals: Pooh himself, Piglet, Kanga and Roo, Tigger and Eeyore. The other characters, Owl, Rabbit and all Rabbit's friends-and-relations down to the smallest beetle, were familiar creatures in the Ashdown Forest, Sussex, where the family lived. Daphne took her husband's dictation – not, as she insisted, that she was qualified to do so, but she must have made an inspiring and amused audience.

There is unfortunately a sad aspect to this apparently idyllic

Right Christopher Robin Milne's original old teddy bear, a first birthday present from his mother in 1920. *Inset* Pooh's fiftieth birthday hum, written by Willa-Jane Addis.

Below E. H. Shepard's original pencil sketch of Christopher Robin and Pooh restoring Eeyore's tail, which Owl had been using as a bell-rope.

family: Christopher Robin grew up rather sour about his youthful fame, probably because he was badly tormented at school by children jealous of his celebrity. He wrote an article denying that he ever had much to do with his father, who, he claimed, did not particularly like children. He said that his mother simply reported nursery life to his father, and that A.A. Milne never told his son the stories before they were published, as described in *We Are Introduced*: instead, his nanny read them to him afterwards. He did however give his father credit for being amusing, original and kind, and, after all, it was not generally the custom in the 1920s to live as closely with one's children as we do now.

Winnie the Pooh is a truly heroic figure, in the old-fashioned sense: he is good and brave and modest. Far from being a bear of very little brain, he has remarkably good ideas in an emergency, such as using an umbrella for a boat to rescue Piglet. Pooh's hums, or poems, are frequently good, and have inspired many original hums ever since. Opposite is a hum written by Willa-Jane Addis to celebrate Pooh's fiftieth birthday in 1979. (She won a great deal of honey in a competition with it.) Some of the best children's book illustrations ever were drawn for Winnie the Pooh by Ernest Shephard. It is astonishing how well he interpreted the characters, and gave life to Christopher Robin's toys. The original drawing of "A Pooh Party" was sold at Sotheby's in 1968 for $1450. A new hum appeared in *Punch* to celebrate:

Pooh's Birthday Hum (1979)
I'm not so young and nifty
On the fourteenth I'll be fifty
So my friends must not be thrifty
On the day

My skin's a little tighter and
My hair is slightly whiter
But I'm sprighter and I'm brighter
Than a jay

I've got a little lumpy
And I'm not so up-and-jumpy
But I'm still quite nice and dumpy
In the tum

My nose is not so furry
And my eyes are rather blurry
But my voice is always purry
When I hum

Though the cars are fast and grumbly
And the towns are big and rumbly
I live in my own bumbly
Kind of way

Isn't it rum
When a Hum won't come?
I ought to be rich – so there!
Isn't it funny
How a bear makes money,
But none of it sticks to the bear?

There are four Walt Disney shorts based on the original stories, and it must be said that they have come in for much criticism from Pooh fans everywhere. Their image of Pooh lacks the bewildered charm of the original, and the director thought that Christopher Robin's longish hair and smock (normal clothes for a boy in 1926) were too sissy! English fans in particular were angry, because Piglet was replaced completely by a very American gopher. It seems a pity to change the original so much, and particularly the hums, but the films do introduce a new audience to the little bear and his friends.

However, the most important thing about Pooh and Christopher Robin is their loving relationship, and the wish fulfillment of having your bear hug you back. The very end of the stories is about parting from your bear as you grow up. Even if you keep him or perhaps have more bears, it is never the same as being a child again:

> "'Pooh, promise you won't forget about me, ever.
> Not even when I'm a hundred.'
> Pooh thought for a little.
> 'How old shall I be then?'
> 'Ninety-nine.'
> Pooh nodded.
> 'I promise,' he said . . ."

Top Some contemporary toys based on A. A. Milne's original characters, *left to right*, Tigger, Pooh, Piglet and Eeyore.

Above The bridge at Hartfield, Sussex, England, where Winnie the Pooh invented the game of Pooh Sticks: ". . . he dropped two (fir-cones) in at once, and leant over the bridge to see which of them would come out first . . ."

Right Frontispiece from H. C. Cradock's *The Best Teddy Bear in the World* (1926), illustrated by Honor C. Appleton.

Left A soft and gentle little toy Pooh by Pedigree, with his indispensable honey jar, and a copy of his adventures by A. A. Milne.

24

We told him not to go beyond the Garden.

HONOR C. APPLETON

All the original toys are now in America: Piglet, Kanga and Roo, Tigger and Eeyore went on a nationwide tour of the States in 1947; they are now displayed in the reception room of E.P. Dutton and Co, 201 Park Avenue South, New York, who publish the books in the US.

A later, but equally famous British bear is Paddington. His creator, Michael Bond, had been longing to call a suitable character after London's Paddington railway station, near which he lived. He was presented with the right bear-er in Selfridge's toy department one Christmas. There on the shelf, left all alone by the Christmas rush, sat a glove puppet teddy bear, with a decided character. Michael Bond bought him for his wife, but teddy was soon providing the basis for the main character in the Paddington stories. They start on Paddington Station, when a little bear, wearing a hat and sitting on a

suitcase, is spotted by a certain Mr Brown. There is a label around the bear's neck saying, "Please Look After This Bear. Thank You." With a storybook logic, the Brown family welcome him into their home, where he lives an independent life, being helpful and willing, but often causing remarkable disasters by mistake. The other characters in the stories provide the perfect foil for him: the 'soft touch' family Brown; Mrs Bird, the housekeeper who is in charge of everything; Mr Gruber, an immigrant like Paddington, and therefore his great friend. Then there is an enemy in the shape of mean Mr Curry next door. The delightful illustrations by Peggy Fortnum add immensely to Paddington's charm.

Originally, Paddington came from Darkest Africa, but Michael Bond's literary agent told him that there were no bears in Africa. Peru, on the other hand, had lots of bears. So although Paddington is really very English, with his battered duffel coat, and love of marmalade, there is always his mysterious past with an aunt in Darkest Peru to fire children's imagination.

Michael Bond has received thousands of letters from admirers of all ages, from all over the world: these are often addressed to Paddington at his fictional address, 32 Windsor Gardens, but they always find their way to the right place. All letters are personally replied to, and Michael Bond signs all the cards himself. This is because he once wrote to the American actress Deanna Durbin, when he was very young, and was dreadfully disappointed when he received a standard printed reply!

The first fan-letter, together with much more information about Paddington, is on display in London, at the Toy and Model Museum, Craven Hill. There is a whole shop devoted to Paddington, called Paddington and Friends, at 22 Crawford Place, London, where you might meet Karen Bond, daughter of the author. She was a little girl when Paddington first became famous, and still loves him to this day.

Facing page, top Michael Bond, creator of Paddington Bear, in his office above the shop Paddington and Friends, 22 Crawford Place, London.

Facing page, bottom Paddington Bear, in characteristic duffel coat and hat, as illustrated by Peggy Fortnum.

Left Paddington Station, London, where Paddington stands in a glass case.

Below The English Paddington soft toy, with his Aunt Lucy, made by Gabrielle Designs of Doncaster.

The character survives so well because Paddington is very definite: he is morally reliable, with a strong sense of right and wrong. He has the innocence of a small child, coupled with adult sophistication and independence. One of Paddington's outstanding characteristics is his ability to go straight to the highest authority in a crisis.

Some bears are designed with merchandizing in mind from the start. This was never so with Paddington, although there is a very good toy teddy bear in his image, complete with hat, duffel coat and Wellington boots. The English version is a firm bear in texture, but the American one is much softer and more cuddly, with a variety of outfits, including a jogging suit. Michael Bond has said that Paddington bears are bought particularly by young girls when they leave home to live in their own apartments. He suspects Paddington might even be seen as a father figure, even though he is permanently only nine years old!

Facing page, top The soft, cuddly, American version of Paddington, by Eden Toys. He has a variety of outfits, including a jogging suit.

Facing page, bottom Paddington and Friends, 22 Crawford Street, London, is a wonderful shop devoted to the little bear. Even the carpet is decorated with bear pictures, and a specialty is marmalade fudge.

Right The immortal story of Goldilocks and the Three Bears, from *Fireside Tales Bedtime Stories of Pixies and Teddy Bears*, illustrated by Willy Shermelé (Purnell Publishing 1979).

Below A page from the *1974 Daily Express Rupert Annual*, containing eight separate adventures in both verse and prose. *Inset* Rupert Bear soft toy by Tebro which says, "I am Rupert Bear. Let's go to sleep now" when you pull his cord.

This page, facing page, top Superted was born in Wales, the product of Mike Young's need to entertain his stepchildren. The little bear started life as a toy factory reject found by extra-terrestrial Spottyman. Spottyman sprinkled magic dust on the bear, and took him to see Mother Nature who gave him a secret word which transforms him at will into Superted. Together the two heroes fly about rescuing people and having adventures, as in this illustration from *Superted and the Pharaoh's Treasure*. The new character has been an enormous success, and the non-violent, loving and moral tales have been bought for showing on Walt Disney cable television.

By this time, SuperTed and Spottyman were flying over the desert, looking for the lost girl. They had been looking for quite a time and had not seen anything. "We'll never find her in all this sand, Spotty."

"We can't just give up, SuperTed," said Spotty. "Think of that poor, lost girl."

As they flew over the dunes, they caught sight of a speck on the horizon. It was the girl's landrover. Close to it, half buried in the sand, they found a small brush. "Let's dig here, Spotty. You never know, we might find the doorway to the tombs." Soon they swept the sand off a large, stone slab. They had found the entrance.

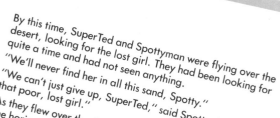

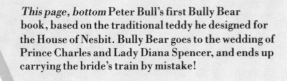

This page, bottom Peter Bull's first Bully Bear book, based on the traditional teddy he designed for the House of Nesbit. Bully Bear goes to the wedding of Prince Charles and Lady Diana Spencer, and ends up carrying the bride's train by mistake!

Peter Bull, actor, traveler, writer, and arctophile pictured with Aloysius, star of *Brideshead Revisited*, and Bully Bear, the teddy he designed for the House of Nesbit. He amassed a collection of over three thousand bears, some of which can be seen in the London Toy and Model Museum, Bayswater.

Chapter 3

Some Famous Bears And Their People

A great many of us were attached to a favorite bear as a child, and although the trusting belief in teddy's listening ear may diminish as we get older, the affection survives. Until recently, however, many adults, particularly men, would find it very difficult to display their treasured old friend without being thought childish, to say the least.

The people in this chapter have braved the ridicule of being "too old" for teddies and have used their enthusiasm for our furry friends for many marvelous purposes. They – and their bears – have provided entertainment and solace, education and fun, to children and adults alike.

Peter Bull, Theodore and Aloysius

Peter Bull, author, actor and traveler, died in 1984, but will be remembered by bear lovers everywhere with intense gratitude. He did much to make teddies not only acceptable, but even desirable. He felt very strongly that it was vital to remember one's childhood and said, "Above all, you were aware that there was always somebody to tell your joys and sorrows to, and in far more cases than I had ever realized, this someone was Teddy Bear."

It all started for Peter Bull when his mother gave his beloved teddy away to a garage sale while he was still at school, considering that at sixteen Peter was too old for toys. He was later to acquire Theodore, a small teddy who fitted conveniently into his pocket, but he felt sure that the shock of losing his first bear was what set him on the path to becoming the champion of all adult arctophiles.

Like a great many people, Peter had always believed teddies to be an English invention. As you know, this is actually not the case. When he realized the facts, he went to America to see what the American people thought of the whole crazy mystique. At first, opinions were hard to come by, but when Peter Bull appeared on the *Today* program one morning in the 1960s, teddy consciousness really took off. Letters poured in from relieved enthusiasts, mostly adults, and Peter immediately noted the difference between British and American attitudes to

Top Theodore, Peter Bull's favorite little companion, with some of his many possessions.

Above Theodore in bed, with a fan letter.

teddies. In Britain the letters were full of childhood memories of nasty brothers' ill-treatment of bears, not to mention various descriptions of fumigation and disinfection which the bears of sick children had received! The American letters were quite different and Peter Bull was astonished by their violence. He couldn't understand how the teddy bear could be responsible for so many dreadful and dramatic problems of a strictly adult nature: feuds, marriage breakdowns, and even suicides.

There were also many letters expressing admiration and gratitude. Little Theodore in particular received personal mail, and many presents, including an even smaller companion who arrived in a soap tin and was known as "H.H." This wasn't the only bear offered to Peter. People all over America saw him as a suitable home for any unwanted bears, or bears they could no longer cope with. He restricted his acceptance to those in real danger of extinction, and received some remarkable examples as a result.

One bear, who spent over fifty years on the shelf of Ladds Dry Goods Store in Saco, Maine, was destined to become a big star. He was an old bear, with a hump, indicating he was probably made before the First World War. His previous owner, Mrs Euphemia Ladd, thought he had acquired it from sitting hunched up on a shelf for so many years! Peter Bull named him Delicatessen, and kept him for twenty years before fame struck. Granada Television in Britain were making the serial of Evelyn Waugh's famous novel *Brideshead Revisited*, in which Aloysius the teddy bear is a prominent character. Naturally, the producer approached Peter Bull about casting the part. Delicatessen turned out to be perfect: the right age and size and in ideal condition. (He did have stiff competition from Big Ted, the family bear of the Howards, in whose ancestral home, Castle Howard, most of the film was made.) Book One of the novel is called *Et In Arcadia Ego*, meaning in Latin: "I too have dwelt in Arcadia." It is interesting that "Arcadia" means "bear country", just as arctophile means friend of the bear!

Aloysius is the constant companion of the beautiful but doomed Lord Sebastian Flyte at Oxford, where he and the narrator, Charles Ryder, are both supposed to be studying. But they spend far more time having fun: "Beyond the gate, beyond the winter garden that was once the lodge, stood an open, two-seater Morris Cowley. Sebastian's teddy bear sat at the

Left Anthony Andrews, who played Lord Sebastian Flyte in the television series of Evelyn Waugh's *Brideshead Revisited*, with Peter Bull's Aloysius.

Below Peter Bull's Bully Bear, worried about his age, and overhearing some young people referring to him as a "dear, old-fashioned bear", becomes a punk rocker, in *Bully Bear Goes Punk!*

wheel. We put him between us – 'Take care he's not sick' – and drove off.'' It is all very charming, and rather sad, because such a lovely existence surely cannot last. Sure enough, poor Sebastian comes to a sad, drunken end. But Delicatessen was perfect in the role of Aloysius, and to celebrate his success, Peter Bull had his name permanently changed by deed poll. When *Brideshead* was shown in America, Aloysius went back to his native land, with Anthony Andrews, who played Sebastian. He was a great success, and received full star treatment, even to the extent of making a paw print in the cement outside Grauman's Chinese Theater in Hollywood! When Aloysius lunched in the *Four Seasons*, one of the smartest restaurants in New York, he was offered a drink by the waiter, and graciously accepted a Vodka Martini much to everyone's amusement. Peter Bull was afraid that success might go to Aloysius' head, but so far he seems as natural as if nothing much had happened since his Delicatessen days.

Before Brideshead fixed him in the public's imagination, a

traditional English toy firm, the House of Nisbet, had approached Peter Bull with a view to making a teddy bear to Peter's specifications. He had long expressed himself dissatisfied with the gimmicky teddies that were on offer to the general public. The basic features which Peter Bull felt to be important were, "....a snout, a hump and that woollen embroidery for the pads and paws. Children like to pick at the embroidery and then it's hell for the poor parent to knit on again."

Delicatessen had all the right features, and the House of Nisbet's "Bully Bear" could be said to be his direct descendent. The new bear star was launched in the British House of Commons in October 1980, at a party attended by members of the House of Lords and the House of Commons. The prototype

Bully Bear was sold at auction in aid of RADAR, a charity for the disabled, to the Marquis of Bath. It was at his family's country home, Longleat, that the largest ever gathering of teddy bears and their friends was held in June 1979.

Peter Bull was inspired by the new teddy to write his *Bully Bear* books, which were illustrated in a lively fashion by Enid Irving. It all begins with Bully Bear being sent to the Royal Wedding in 1981, to carry Lady Diana's train. He has other adventures, including becoming a punk rocker for a while and going to Hollywood because he was a bit jealous of Aloysius! Peter Bull described his character: "he is greedy, rather a snob, is always in the right (or so he thinks!) and runs a respectable teddy bear's Lodging House in Chelsea . . . Bully has a kind of endearing naïveté and naughtiness which has made him very

Above Teddy Edward on top of the world, with Sherpa girls near Mount Everest in the Himalayas.

Facing page, top Teddy Edward, the intrepid traveler, sits looking out of the airplane window, on the way to yet another exotic adventure with Patrick and Molly Matthews.

Facing page, bottom Teddy Edward winning his famous skiing medal in the snowy Alps, which he always wears.

Facing page, far right Yogi Bear, Hanna-Barbara's famous cartoon bear who, together with his little side-kick Boo Boo, raids the pic-a-nic baskets of unwary tourists in Jellystone Park.

Gina Campbell, daughter of the late Sir Donald Campbell, follows in her father's footsteps, both in trying to break world speed records, and in having the same good luck mascot, Mr Woppit, who survived her father's fatal crash.

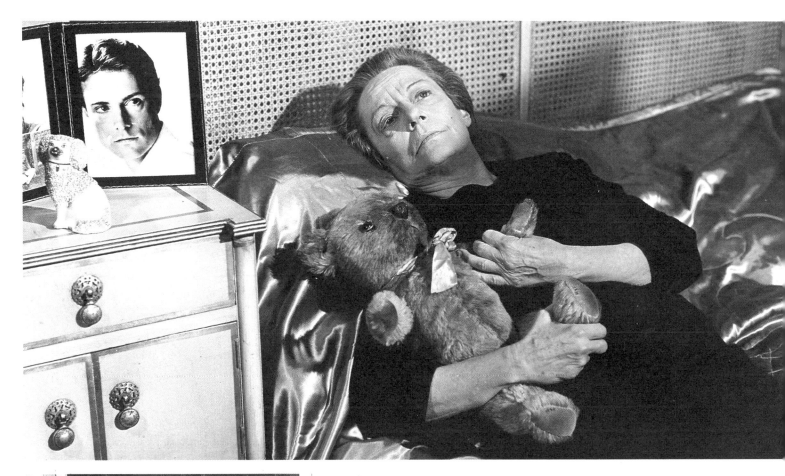

popular . . ." Peter also wrote some general teddy books, the last of which was *A Hug of Teddy Bears*, published in the USA by E.P. Dutton. The House of Nisbet has created three different sizes of Bully Bear: Bully himself, Young Bully, who is smaller, and wears the regalia of the Worshipful Company of Peanut Butter Eaters(!), and Bully Minor, who is an endearing fluffy baby bear.

Peter Bull will be sadly missed by arctophiles everywhere. No Teddy Bear Event, Tea Party, Picnic or Concert is quite complete without him.

Top Tallulah Bankhead, in *Die, Die My Darling* (1965), fanatically clutches her teddy bear, while keeping Stephanie Powers under lock and key.

Left Outside 10 Downing Street, London, home of British Prime Ministers, sits Humphrey, teddy bear of Mrs Thatcher. He is waiting to be picked up by his friends Annabel Bear and Fred the Ted, who are all going to a Teddy Bear's Picnic at Belvoir Castle.

Patrick Matthews and Teddy Edward

Patrick Matthews is the official photographer of Teddy
Edward, an appealing British bear, very popular with younger
children. Patrick and his wife Mollie, who writes the books,
have been taken to more than twenty one countries by their
adventurous little friend, who has earned himself the title of
"Much Traveled Bear". The original Teddy Edward belonged

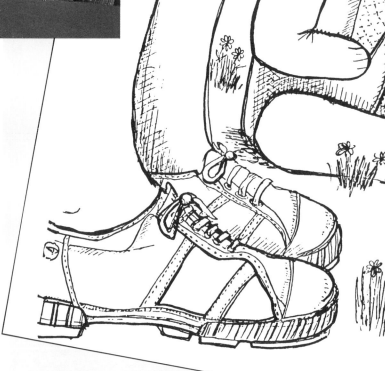

to Sarah Matthews, aged two, but he became somewhat
battered, and another bear of the same kind was purchased.
The two bears were sent to a dolls' hospital, and Teddy Edward
Mark II emerged, after plastic surgery, looking as similar as
possible to Teddy Edward Mark I. The new bear does all the
traveling and posing now, while his predecessor leads a
comfortably retired life in Sarah's bedroom.

Meanwhile, the new Teddy Edward was winning his specially
designed medal in a ski race, and appearing on television in
countries as far apart as New Zealand and Albania, as well as
being very popular in Britain. The little bear has made some
fabulous journeys. He took a five hundred mile trip down the
River Niger in Africa, to Timbuktu in the Sahara Desert.
(Teddy Edward was slightly worried about what to wear in such
a hot place, as he obviously could not take off his fur coat.) The
local people were very interested in him, although a little
frightened. They thought he was a small lion, as there are no
bears in Africa.

Having been to one of the hottest places in the world, it was
inevitable that Teddy Edward should then want to see the
highest, Mount Everest, and the deepest, the Grand Canyon in
Colorado. He traveled all over Arizona, Colorado and New
Mexico, and went to New York, where he was photographed in
front of some of the famous sights. He has been to so many
places that there is now an informative atlas for young children,
called *Around the World with Teddy Edward.* Teddy Edward is
a great friend of Peter Bull's bear Theodore.

Above left The Marquis of Bath, who lives with his
teddy bear Clarence at Longleat.

Below Peter Bull's book *Bully Bear at the Teddy Bear Rally* describes one small bear's experience at the unique first large gathering of arctophiles and their friends at Longleat. Peter Bull said, "In this adventure, being rather a snob, he sucks up to Clarence, Lord Bath's bear."

...pot to eat an ice ...me of Attractions.

He heard a voice.
"Hallo Old Chap" it said, "Had a run in with Jumbo, I hear."
It was Clarence (who owned the Marquess of Bath). "Elephants have no place at a Bears' Bank Holiday" Bully snorted "I shall complain to the Management"

41

Russell McLean and his hospital bears

Some very fine people love teddy bears, and have used their interest in constructive and helpful ways. One such person was the late Russell McLean of Ohio, the original "Teddy Bear Man". He had been in the hospital frequently as a child, and knew how frightening and lonely it was. He realized that the friendly face of a teddy bear would have helped him, and he decided to supply as many children as possible with a brand new teddy bear, to comfort them on their first night in hospital. He was helped by a local broadcaster, Easter Straker, who had a daily television show for children. Any child on the show with a birthday would give a dollar towards buying the bears. Money poured in from all sides for such an obviously good idea, and it became much easier to persuade a child into hospital in Lima, Ohio. Russell McLean ran the whole project himself, and before he was forced to retire, presented his fifty-thousandth teddy bear to a deserving child. There is something remarkable about teddy bears. The children greeted the new bear as an old friend and comforter, even when they had left their own favorite toys at home. Those parents who sadly could not take their children home afterwards would perhaps be a little comforted by having teddy to remember the child by.

In 1973, McLean's idea was expanded by James T. Ownby of Honolulu into Good Bears of the World, an organization which supplies teddy bears not only to children in hospitals and institutions, but to anyone else of any age who needs the comfort of a teddy while hospitalized. If you wish to join, write to The Good Bears of the World, P.O. Box 8236, Honolulu, Hawaii, 96815, enclosing a stamped self-addressed envelope. Many bear

42

Some Famous Bears And Their People

bear lent by
MASTER PETER PHILLIPS, SON OF
R.H PRINCESS ANNE & CAPTAIN MARK PHILLIPS.

lovers belong to the organization and have a great time getting in contact with friendly people, while doing a lot of good to children. The annual membership fees are used to buy the teddies and distribute the newsletter, *Bear Tracks*.

Facing page, top The Ewoks, space teddy bears of the film *The Return of the Jedi*, proved to be so popular that the next film *Caravan of Courage* was devoted to them.

Facing page, An Ewok soft toy, by Palitoy.

Top The Prince and Princess of Wales, with their first son, William, and his koala bear.

Left Master Peter Phillips, son of Princess Anne and Captain Mark Phillips, kindly lent his teddy bear to an exhibition at Longleat.

Chapter 4

Distinguished members of London arctophile John Carrie's collection, including Rupture, whose squeaker has gone, at the front.

Collecting Bears

*My teddy bear
has short, gold hair,
a rather squashed nose,
and little black toes . . .*

Real arctophiles usually only have room in their hearts for one special teddy bear, probably the friend of their childhood. But this does not stop them from accumulating whole "hugs" (the official collective term for a group of teddies) of others to keep the first one company. There are various ways of achieving a satisfactory hug: mostly you cannot help it as, if other people discover your interest, you are quite likely to find yourself overwhelmed with no-longer-needed teddies looking for a good home. Some people collect only the rather valuable older teddies, while others open their arms to any bear who happens by. Whatever you do, make sure you feel comfortable with their personalities. A teddy bear has his character formed by the people he has known before and sometimes they might not be all that easy to live with!

Peter Bull was given a valuable "Peter" bear by an admirer. These are very rare, as they were made only between 1925 and 1928 by the Gebruder Sussenguth factory near Coburg in Germany. They are realistic looking bears, with rolling glass eyes, opening mouths with moving tongues and sharp wooden teeth. They have loud and realistic growlers, and when sent through the mail, the parcels were often opened to see if what they contained was alive! They did not last very long, because, in spite of their genial expressions, they frightened children out of their minds. Peter Bull had to sell Peter Bear in the end, as he proved to be an uncomfortable creature to live with.

Teddy bears will not qualify as proper "antiques" until 2002, when they will be one hundred years old. But there has been a great deal of interest recently in collecting what might well be called vintage teddies. So much so, in fact, that the big auction houses are taking them to put in special sales, and the older ones fetch high prices. There is also a growing number of specialist shops and fairs where arctophiles gather together to pick up advice, add to their collections and admire other people's

treasures. *The Bazaar des Bears*, a teddy shop in historic Pike Place, Seattle, Washington, has been made famous by owner Michelle Durkson Clise's delightful books, *My Circle of Bears* and *Ophelia's World* (Clarkson N. Potter Inc). The books are illustrated with Marsha Burns' beautiful photographs of the bears dressed in antique costumes and surrounded by pretty and interesting objects.

If you wish to put a price on a teddy bear, an invaluable book is *The Teddy Bear Catalog* by Peggy & Alan Bialosky (Workman Publishing Company Inc). It contains pictures and descriptions of all kinds of bears, together with their current prices.

The original teddy bear had a hump on his back, a pointy nose, and larger back legs, to look more like a real bear. He had long arms and legs with large paws and feet, sometimes sewn with black wool toes. His arms and legs were jointed at hip and shoulder, his head swiveled, and his eyes were often metal shoe buttons, or glass on wire. He was made of real mohair plush, or sometimes velvet, and felt quite firm, as he was stuffed with wood wool or straw. Sometimes he had a growler, or bells in his ears.

Above John Carrié, London teddy bear collector, pictured with some of his huge hug: "You put them down, and they fall into such delightful attitudes!"

Left Mary Batchelor, whose son Michael started her collection of over 1,500 teddy bears, which overflow her small Wiltshire cottage. The most famous is Oliver, sitting at the top in an armchair. He is a very well-traveled bear, with his own passport which has been stamped in many countries.

The most valuable bears are marked with the maker's name. For instance, a good Steiff bear will still have his button in his ear. It is very difficult to tell who the maker is of an unmarked bear, as so many were made in tiny workrooms dotted all over America, Germany and, since the First World War, Britain. Any unusual features will raise the price, such as spots or stripes, a good costume, a working growler or squeaker, or a particularly sweet expression.

"Well-worn teddies which have been beat up, sucked on, played with, and loved are worth the most to me," according to New York collector Susan Kelner Freeman. She owns about sixty toy bears, each named and with a full wardrobe. Mrs Motorman, a distinguished member of her collection, has her own money in French francs, as Mrs Freeman insists that she only spends money when in France.

There is a quarterly magazine, *The Teddy Bear and Friends* (Hobby House Press, Cumberland MD 21502), through which you can trade bears with other arctophiles.

I took my own little bear to see Bunny Campione, the Teddy Bear expert, at Sotheby's, London. She liked him very much, and told me that he was probably English, but might be American, and that he dated from about 1910. She pointed out that he had had a hump at one time, but that someone had stitched it down to give him a straight back! His fur is rubbed off, he has no eyes, and his squeaker is long since silent, but he is apparently worth about $40! I thought that this was a lot of money to spend on someone else's old toy; although of course his real value is incalculable.

Sotheby's, London, will accept bears made before about 1930. The condition does not matter as much as for a doll, but a

Top Baron Herr Doktor Bernhardt von Baerburg of Berne, chief bear in Nesta Wynn Ellis's collection. He is a banker bear, and his city suit was made by Moto, a top Savile Row tailor.

Above Nesta Wynn Ellis with a small part of her international collection. Each of the 28 bears has a name and distinct personality: "Bears make life more bearable. They are remarkable company when one is alone."

well-preserved bear is likely to fetch more than a worn one. A teddy bear's character can raise his price: an original Steiff bear, wearing a cardboard boater and a bow tie, neither of which were original, looked so jaunty that he fetched $950! Sotheby's sold a little black fluffy bear, with an unusual look, and big ears, for $430. He had belonged to a ninety-year-old lady who had owned him since she was a baby, so he wasn't really a teddy bear at all, more of a pre-Teddy. When Twentieth Century-Fox were clearing out their Hollywood studios in 1978, they sold a dark brown teddy bear who had appeared in the film *Captain January* with Shirley Temple, for $450. A really good teddy bear can now command as much as $1,000!

Teddy bears are rather unassuming creatures. They are companions and confidantes, and any gimmick tends to get in the way of their true function. The most reliable teddies are undoubtedly variations on the original one. The basic

characteristics are: animal colored plush (anything from white, through the beiges and golds, to brown and black); jointed shoulders and hips, and a swiveling head (teddy should be able to sit down, stand up, turn to look at you, and wave his arms about in a friendly manner); glass or button eyes; and a nice black stitched nose, mouth and toes.

A relatively new development in the bear market are realistic-looking bears, although they can however hardly be

Left Traditional humpback teddy, by Merrythought: number 145 of a limited collector's edition of 1,000, made especially for Hamleys, London.

Above Sotheby's auctioneer teddy, photographed to celebrate the teddy bear's new value in the sale rooms of Britain and America.

Facing page International postcards from Rose Wharnsby's vast teddy bear postcard collection.

St. Valentine's Day Greetings.

O BEAR WITH THIS TRUE HEART OF MINE
AND BE MY FAITHFUL VALENTINE!

"POOR OLD TEDDY!"

Wishing you a glorious 4th"

Above Rufus Bears by Canterbury Bears: unjointed and soft, they tumble about.

defined at teddies. These tend to be soft, so that they sit or lie down like their living models. Pandas and polar bears are often like this. The slightly human quality of a true teddy is missing, but they are nevertheless very cuddly.

Steiff have opened a museum in their old factory at Giengen-on-the-Brenz, where their toys are still made. The toys on display cover the whole one hundred years since the company was founded, including the little felt elephant which started the whole thing. To mark the upsurge of interest in collecting antique toys, Steiff have produced replicas of some of their most popular playthings. These include a silver-gray reproduction of "Friend Petz", the first bear.

High-tech Petsy bear is the latest in a long and distinguished line. He retains original features, but is softer and can go in the washing machine. Steiff also makes gold-plated jointed teddy bear jewelery, including teddy earrings!

In 1983, Care Bears burst upon the scene. They are the very opposite of the discreet teddy bear, with his non-committal expression, developed by years of affection into an individual character. Care Bears are mass marketed with mass appeal in mind, and as well as the soft toys, there are poseable plastic figures, stationery, cartoons, books, T-shirts . . . and practically everything else you can think of. They are a rather frivolous bunch, with pastel plush, heart-shaped plastic noses, heart-shaped paws, and a "tummy graphic" illustrating their characters. They have a whole mystique of their own, living in a cloudy country, among the rainbows, called Care-a-Lot.

There are thirteen Care Bears, with names like Good Luck Bear (a bright green bear, with a shamrock on his tummy, and a winking eye), Funshine Bear (yellow, with a smiling sun), and Grumpy Bear (dark blue, with a cloud raining pink hearts). It could be said that they over-state the obvious role of the teddy, but it cannot be denied that they are both pretty and cuddly.

It was inevitable, of course, that one day a teddy would go into space. The first was the Russian Mishka, in his cartoon. But the third film in the Star Wars series, *The Return of the Jedi*, introduced the Ewoks, appealing allies of the rebel heroes. They are a brave and chivalrous tribe of little furry creatures which live in large tree camps.

They have all the characteristics attributed to teddies, in the

Above Giant Rufus Snow Bear, by Canterbury Bears, designed specifically for cuddling.

Left Oxford, a small North American humpback bear, made by Canterbury Bears, won top prize at the first Great Western Bear Convention in San José in 1983.

Left This picture disk, with an authentic early recording of the Teddy Bear's Picnic, comes with membership of the International Teddy Bear Club.

Left, above, and top right The New Year's Teddy Bears' Concert at the Barbican Centre, London, attracted thousands of bears. Human representatives from all aspects of beardom came along too.

way of being thoroughly good and kind, and helping the human characters in their fight against injustice. So popular have they proved to be that they were given the next film in the series, *Caravan of Courage*, all to themselves. It is now possible to buy soft toys modelled on the various Ewok characters – Wicket W. Warrick, Princess Kneesa, Paploo, etc – they have turned a full circle, and gone back to being teddy bears!

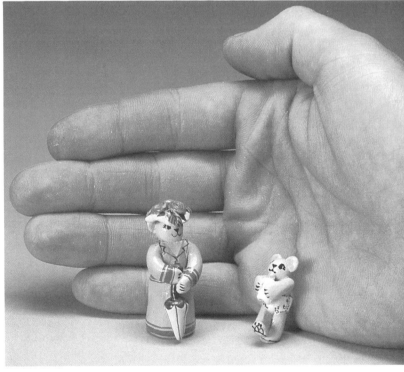

Top The Zodiac Bears, designed by Peter Bull and Pauline McMillan for House of Nisbet. The bears live in an English village called Little Ticking, where they hold regular Bear Day celebrations, to which each bear contributes according to astrological personality.

Above Soft fully-dressed bears, above left, by Benson's Cuddly Toys of Birmingham, England.

Above Small ceramic bears by Ursa Minor, Cilgeraint House, Saint Ann's Bethesda, Gwyned, North Wales. They are hand-modeled and individually painted, so each one is unique.

This page The Wareham Bears are a busy community of about one hundred bears who have come from all over the world to settle in the cellar of 18 Church Street, Wareham, Dorset, England. They built themselves a house with stabling, then a shop, a garden, a tennis court and a rugby football field. They even have a maltings to make their own beer. Scrum, *right*, is the life and soul of the community, and plays rugby for the Bearbarians against the All Blues. He owes his superb physique to vigorous exercise and pork pies. The Wareham Bears' house, *below*: the bears are always very busy coming and going, but would be happy to be visited between March and September.

Facing page An unusual early dark brown bear, with characteristically large paws, and a sweet intelligent expression, sold at Sotheby's in 1984.

Facing page Some bears on the stairs on sale at John Carrié's antique shop at 32 Pembridge Road, London.

Above A guardsbear by Merrythought all present and correct to defend Her Majesty the Queen.

Left The Standard Bearer, Rose Wharnsby's postcard of a guardsbear.

THE STANDARD BEARER

Facing page Hamley bears by Merrythought, on parade up Regent Street, London in front of Hamleys, one of the best toy shops in the world.

Above A tumbling hug of mixed teddy bears, on sale at Hamleys, Regent Street, London.

Left Jubilee Bear, four foot high, specially created by Tony Toys of Brighton, England, to celebrate their twentieth anniversary. There is a limited edition of 200 individually-numbered American bears on sale in the USA.

Above A Yeoman of the Guard teddy bear, by Merrythought, on guard outside the Tower of London.

Right Teddy Susan, a very old bear made of sheepskin, looks at herself in the mirror of an antique bamboo washstand.

Facing page The Alresford bears form a traditional wedding group outside St James's Church (c. 1190) in Surrey, England.

Above Polar bears, by Merrythought, straight from the Arctic.

Left Care Bears, by Palitoy, live in Care-a-Lot, a cloudy country among the rainbows.

Facing page A selection of panda bear teddies, the largest by Vera Small, with the real panda's favorite food: bamboo.

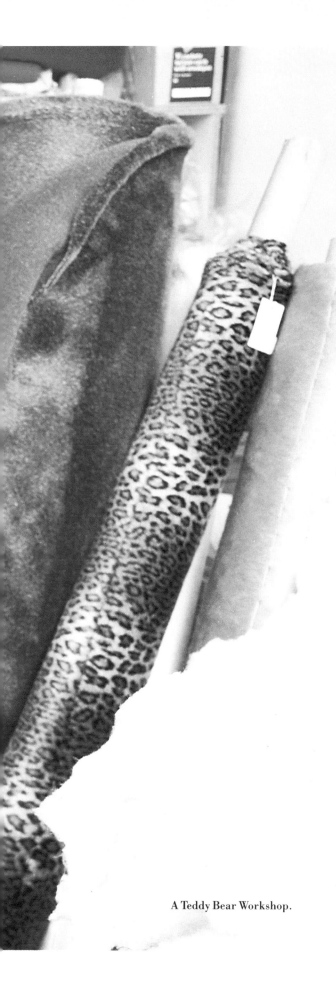

Chapter 5

A Teddy Bear Workshop.

Handmade Bears

You will probably spot many hand-made bears with delightfully individual characters if you haunt church bazaars, craft shows and so on. But why not try your hand at making your own little bear? However simple his design, he will always be the most personal bear of all. And even the most complicated patterns are really very easy to manage. There are many to choose from, including Vogue, McCall's Crafts, who have patterns to make a whole family of Berenstain Bears, as well as Brooke Shields' Moon Bears; and Simplicity who have Majorie Puckett's button-jointed bears, and the delightful Vanessa-Ann Collection bears, with their funny faces.

Whatever pattern you choose, of course, the final result is entirely up to you. You do not have to follow the picture on the envelope. Be creative, use the pattern pieces as a basis for your own invention. They will give you a basic shape, which you can then alter or add to as you wish. I have included an elegant French Teddy Bear knitting pattern in this book, for those of you who can knit. Good luck, have fun, and whatever you do, do not leave your needle – or anything else – in the bear. If you cannot find stuffing easily, then old clean nylon panty hose, cut into bits, will be fine.

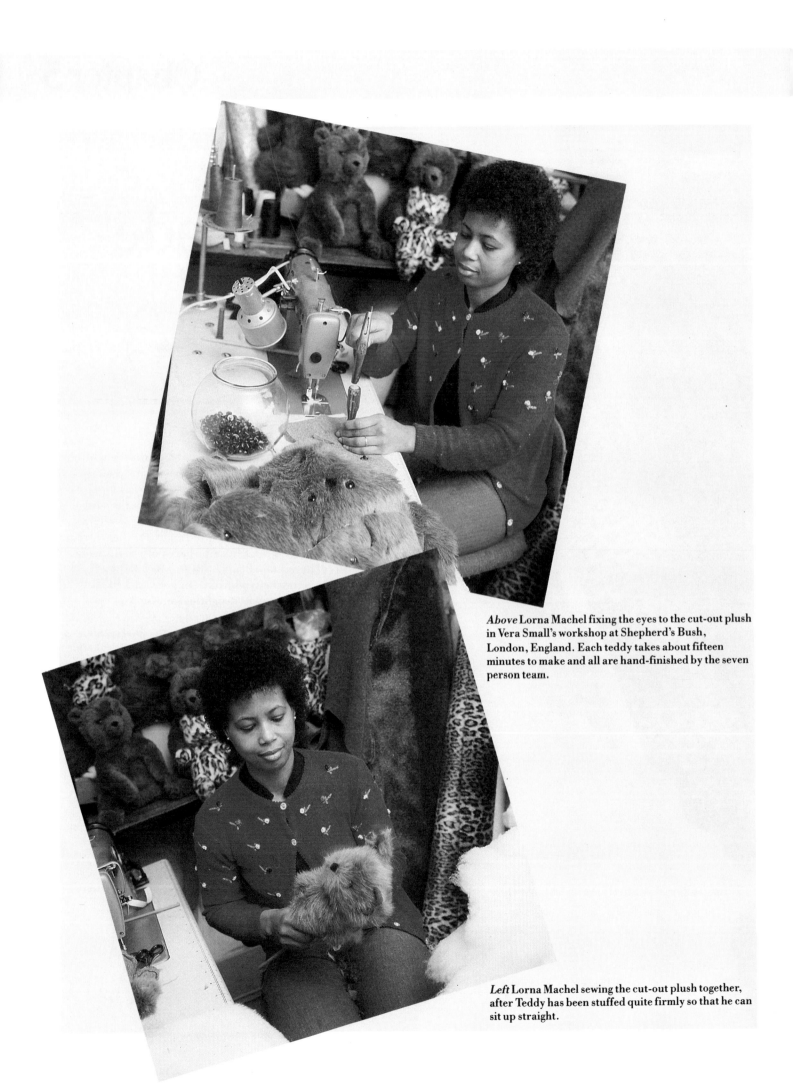

Above Lorna Machel fixing the eyes to the cut-out plush in Vera Small's workshop at Shepherd's Bush, London, England. Each teddy takes about fifteen minutes to make and all are hand-finished by the seven person team.

Left Lorna Machel sewing the cut-out plush together, after Teddy has been stuffed quite firmly so that he can sit up straight.

Handmade Bears

Left Vera Small's unique leopard spotted teddies tumbling around in the stuffing.

Below Vera Small's realistic brown teddy bears in a mountainous spring landscape.

Knitted Ted

The large bear measures 15 in. The small bear measures 10¼ in.

Materials

Small bear: Pingouin "Oued": used double: 2 balls in Blanc No. 27; several strands in Rose No. 26, Daim No. 13, Feu No. 17. 1 pair No. 2 needles. 2 buttons for the eyes. Stuffing.

Large bear: Pingouin "Mohair": used double: 6 balls in Bonbon No. 309; several strands in Glacier No. 322. Negre No. 320. Cerise No. 317. 1 Pair No. 4 needles. 2 buttons for the eyes. Stuffing.

Stitches used

Reverse Stocking Stitch: *purl 1 row, knit 1 row*.

Instructions — Small bear

Legs: Using Blanc, cast on 17 sts and work 1 row, then inc. 1 st at each end of every other row (twice). Work 2 rows straight, then inc. 1 st at each end of next row. Work 2 rows straight, then shape the foot: Work on the last 8 st only working the first 2 sts together on the first row, the first 3 sts together on the 2nd row and the first 2 sts together on the 3rd row, cast off rem. sts.

Rejoin yarn to the sts at center of work. Cont. work beginning with a purl row. Inc. 1 st at the end of row (heel edge), work 1 row straight, work 2 rows dec. 1 st at each row end, work 16 rows straight, work 2 rows dec. 1 st at each row end, 1 row straight, then 4 rows dec. 1 st at each row end, 2 rows straight, 4 rows dec. 1 st at each row end. Cast off rem. sts.

Work a 2nd section in same way, reversing all shapings for the other side of the leg. Then work another leg in same way.

Sole: Using Rose, cast on 6 sts and work 1 row, then inc. 1 st at each end of every other row (twice). Work 6 rows straight then dec. 1 st at each end of every other row (3 times). Cast off.

Arms: Inside section: Using Rose, cast on 7 sts and work 1 row, then inc. 1 st at each end of every other row (3 times). At the same time, beginning on the 5th row, work the last 3 sts in Blanc and work 1 extra st in Blanc from the sts in Rose on every row until all the sts are in Blanc. Throughout this work, work 2 rows straight, then at right hand side of work dec. 1 st on every 4th row (3 times), inc. 1 st on every 4th row (twice), work 8 rows straight, then dec. on every other row as folls: 1 st (twice) 2 st (once). At the same time, at left hand side of work inc. 1 st on every other row (twice), work 2 rows straight, inc. 1 st on every alt. row (once), work 12 rows straight, dec. 1 st on every 4th row (3 times), 2 st on every 2nd row (twice). Cast off rem. sts.
Work a 2nd inside section in same way, reversing all shapings.
For the outer section, work one piece in same way, using Blanc, then work a 2nd piece in same way, reversing all shapings.

Body: Using Blanc, cast on 12 sts and work 1 row, then inc. at right hand side of work (front edge) on every other row as folls: 3 st (once), 2 st (once), 3 st (once) and at the same time, at left hand side of work (back edge): 1 st (twice), 2 st (once). Then inc. 1 st at each end of every other row (4 times), then 1 st at each end of every 4th row (3 times). Work 8 rows straight, then dec. at each end of every other row as folls: 1 st (once), work 4 rows straight, then dec. 1 st at each end of every other row (once), work 4 rows straight, then dec. 1 st at right hand side of work at beg. of row only (once), work back across row without dec. at left hand side of work, work 2 rows straight, then cast off at right hand side of work on every other row as folls: 1 st (6 times), 2 st (twice), 1 st (once), and at the same time, at left hand side of work: 1 st (once), work 4 rows straight, then dec. 1 st on every 4th row (twice), 1 st on every 2nd row (twice). Cast off rem sts. Work a 2nd section in same way, reversing all shapings.

Right side of head: Using Blanc, cast on 17 sts and work 1 row, then inc. at right hand side of work on every other row as folls: 1 st (once), 2 st (once) and 1 st (7 times). At the same time, at left hand side of work, inc. 1 st on every other row (once). 1 st on every 4th row (3 times). After the last inc. on right hand side of work, work 4 rows straight, then to shape the nose, cont. on the first 5 sts only: on the 1st row, dec. 1 st at center front edge of work, then inc. at right hand side of work as folls: 1 st on every other row (3 times), and at the same time, dec. 1 st at left hand side of work (3 times). Cast off rem. sts. Rejoin yarn to the sts left on spare needle, dec. the first st at center edge of work, then dec. at right hand side of work on every other row as folls: 3 st (once), 1 st (once), work 2 rows, then dec. on every

other row as folls: 1 st (3 times), 2 st (once). At the same time, at left hand side of work, work 2 rows straight, then dec. on every other row as folls: 1 st (4 times), 2 st (once), 3 st (once). Cast off rem. sts. Work a 2nd section in same way, reversing all shapings.

Top of Head: Begin with the nose. Using Blanc, cast on 5 sts. Work 8 rows straight, then inc. at each end of row as folls: 1 st on every other row (5 times), 1 st on every 4th row (4 times). Work 16 rows straight, then dec. 1 st at each end of every 4th row (4 times), then 1 st on every 2nd row (6 times). Cast off rem. sts.

Ears: Using Blanc, cast on 12 sts and work 3 rows, then cont. as folls: 4th row: work 1 st, *work twice into the next st, work 2 sts*. Work 7 rows straight, then change to Col. Rose and cont. in rev. st st on wrong side of the section in Blanc. Work 2 rows straight, then work as folls: work 1 st,* work 2 sts tog., work 2 sts*. Work 2 rows straight. Using 2 double ended needles, place half of the sts on each needle and cast off, working 1 stitch from each needle together. Work a 2nd ear in same way.

Nose: Using Daim, cast on 4 sts. Work 3 rows, then inc. 2 sts at each end of next row. Work 1 row, then dec. 1 st at each end of next row. Cast off.

To make up

Join the 2 sections of the legs and the sole, then the 2 sections of the arms leaving the end open. Stuff. Stitch the opening. Join the 2 sections of the body, leaving an opening. Stuff. Stitch the opening. Join the 3 sections of the head, leaving an opening. Stuff. Stitch the opening. Sew nose and ears in place. Sew on buttons for the eyes. Embroider the mouth. Stitch the head to the body. Stitch the legs and arms in place.

Instructions — Large bear

Follow the same instructions for the small bear. The different yarns and needles alone change the size of the bear.

Legs: Use Bonbon.

Sole: Use Glacier.

Arms: Begin with Glacier and continue with Bonbon. Work the other section in Glacier.

Body: Use Bonbon.

Head: Use Bonbon.

Top of head: Use Bonbon.

Ears: Begin with Bonbon and cont. with Glacier.

Nose: Use Negre.

Shaggy Bear

Shaggy Bear

Size: About 14½″ tall, standing.

Materials: Unger's Gespa (fringe-like bulky yarn), two (3½ ounce) skeins camel; aluminium crochet hook size P; polyester fiberfill stuffing; large-eyed tapestry needle; two 18mm sew-on animal eyes; green dotted or red satin ribbon 3″ wide, 1¼ yards; several yards of black mohair yarn for embroidering nose and mouth.

Gauge: 1st = 1″. To save time, take time to check gauge.

Body: Starting at lower edge, ch 2.
Rnd 1: Work 7 sc in first ch made. Do not join rnds. Use a marker; move marker each rnd.
Rnd 2: Work 2 sc in each sc around (14 sc). Work even on 14 sc for 5½″ more. Stuff body firmly.
Decrease Rnd 1: Work 2 sts together 7 times. Break off. Leave top edge open for neck edge.

Head: Ch 2.
Rnd 1: Work 5 sc in first ch made.
Rnds 2 & 3: Work 2 sc in each sc around. Join with sl st. Break off.
Make another piece in same manner. Using a length of matching yarn, sew or crochet both head pieces together leaving a small opening. Stuff firmly, then sew opening closed. Sew head securely to body.

Snout: Ch 2.
Rnd 1: Work 7 sc in first ch made.

Rnd 2: Sc in each sc around. Join with sl st to first sc of rnd. Break off leaving an 8″ end. Position on lower portion of head as shown in photograph; sew in place.

Ears: Make 2. Starting at lower edge, ch 3.
Rnd 1: Work 1 sc in 2nd ch from hook, sc in next ch. Break off. Sew to seam at top of head.

Legs: Make 2. Starting at lower edge, ch 2.
Rnd 1: Work 6 sc in first ch made. Working in rnds, work even on 6 sc until leg measures 3½″ from beginning, turn.
Short Row 1: Sc in each of next 3 sc, turn.
Short Row 2: Sc in each of next 2 sc, turn.
Short Row 3: Sc in next sc. Break off. Stuff leg firmly and sew to body so the short rows extend up the side of the body.

Arms: Make 2. Starting at lower edge, ch 2.
Rnd 1: Work 5 sc in first ch made. Working in rnds, work even on 5 sc until the arm measures 3″ from beginning. Break off. Stuff and sew to body.

Finishing: Sew eyes in place. With tapestry needle and black mohair yarn, embroider nose and mouth as shown in photograph: satin-stitch a triangular nose; work mouth in a fly stitch with a straight stitch at each end following pattern. Tie ribbon around bear's neck and make a pretty bow.

Taken from:
Crocheting Teddy Bears
by Barbara Jacksier and Ruth Jacksier
Dover Publications Inc, 1984

Vogue Craft Patterns teddy bears, designed by Linda Carr: There is the basic teddy pattern (no 8658) plus patterns for outfits for every occasion: formal wear, with smart tartan cummerbund; jogging kit, plus sports bag; sleepytime outfit, including night cap and robe; and smart tweed overalls for everyday, plus cap, bow tie, shirt and felt shoes.

Chapter 6

Teddies And Children

My teddy bear
Goes with me everywhere:
Work-time, play-time,
Rough and tumble everyday-time.
And when night falls,
My little Ted,
Snuggles up
With me in bed . . .

There is no denying that teddy bears were originally designed for children. No matter how much affection we retain for our furry friends now, it was only when we were children we really had the ability to give a teddy life. A bonding process takes place between a child and his teddy. They sleep in the same bed, and generally see a great deal of one another, so gradually the bear becomes indispensable. Children are strange, primitive, complicated creatures, full of rituals and beliefs, wild imaginings and ingenious games. And children *do* see their bears as living, however roughly they might sometimes treat them.

"Here is Edward Bear, coming downstairs now,
bump, bump, bump, on the back of his head,
behind Christopher Robin. It is, as far as he knows,
the only way of coming downstairs, but sometimes
he feels that there really is another way, if only he
could stop bumping for a moment and think of it . . ."

Thus Winnie the Pooh is introduced to us at the beginning of A.A. Milne's famous book. Once the two of them are downstairs, the teddy is treated with the greatest respect, and Christopher Robin asks his father to "very sweetly" tell Winnie the Pooh a story, "About himself, because he's *that* sort of Bear." Which shows you exactly how most children feel: their Teddies exist on a different plane, at the same time living and inanimate.

When my own brother was small, he had two beloved teddies called Simon and Cherry. His whole life was lived in relation to them: how they felt, what they wanted to do, eat, see. When he was six, he suddenly realized that they were more durable than he, that they might still be alive after he died. He became very worried and puzzled over what he could do to secure their future. Soon afterwards, however, he went away to boarding school, and gradually lost his urgent interest in the bears he left behind.

Children understand very well the bond between another child and his teddy, and know that the very worst thing that they can do to him is to hurt his little friend. Sometimes, of course, this instinctive knowledge can be used to their own advantage. Practically everyone I have spoken to has mentioned a particular torture inflicted by another child:

"My brother told me that teddy's hair would grow again, and he trimmed his tummy until it was bald with the nail scissors."

"My sister used to bite my teddy's ear, until I screamed for mercy."

"Some horrible children at school threw my teddy out of the window. I ran downstairs, and he was lying face down in a puddle. I cried."

But one poor little girl, now grown up, has not really recovered to this day from seeing a customs official cutting open her teddy bear at the airport to see if he was hiding any illegal goods. An innocent-looking teddy clasped in the arms of an appealing child was a very popular place for hiding smuggled drugs, and unfortunately his fate is a common one for traveling teddies.

This page and facing page New Year 1985 was celebrated in London by a special Teddy Bear's Concert, given at the Barbican Centre. Everyone brought their teddies, including the London Concert Orchestra. The music ranged from the Teddy Bears' Picnic (of course) through the Three Bear Suite to Pineapple Poll and Orpheus in the Underworld. Many distinguished bears appeared in person, including Winnie the Pooh, and Baloo the Bear from the *Jungle Book*. Minuetting Bears danced to the Minuetto Allegretto from Mozart's Symphony No 39.

Previous page The best place for a tired bear after a busy day at Longleat – a lift home on his friend's back.

But that is the bad news. There is a great deal of good news about teddies and children. I have already mentioned Good Bears of the World, the organization which provides teddies to children, and others in need of them, in hospitals and institutions. One little boy was in the hospital for a few days after a mild road accident. He wasn't badly hurt physically, but he would not open his left eye. The doctors could find no reason for this, and attributed it to shock. His parents were very worried about him, naturally. Then someone thought of tucking a teddy bear into the little boy's left arm. First he felt it, and then very slowly, his left eye opened to look at his new friend. After that, he was fine.

The teddy bear was invented just at the right time for maximum popularity. There was a new appreciation of the value of soft toys in child development, as it was realized that loving a teddy bear would help the child to feel kindly towards living animals. Teddy, being particularly special, has survived tides of novelties and other crazes which looked in danger of swamping him. In spite of opposition from all sorts of unlikely sources, he is still triumphantly with us, and more popular than ever.

The International Teddy Bear Club

When Patti Sands was thirteen, she had a curious experience. She had just gone to bed, with her teddy bear lying by her side. Because of her age, she was rather losing interest in toys, and only took him to bed out of habit. Well, teddy obviously decided that he must remind her forcibly of his existence, because he apparently rose to his feet, walked across her chest, and lay down on the other side. After that, needless to say, Patti was more attached to her bear than ever. And when he was stolen,

Facing page, top The Royal National Lifeboat Institution teddy bear attended the Teddy Bears' Picnic at Richmond, England.

Facing page, bottom A family of teddy bears and people dressed in antique costume at the Teddy Bears' Picnic at Richmond, England.

Above A teddy bear protected from the rain with his own miniature umbrella at the Teddy Bears' Picnic, Richmond, England.

Left Adventurous teddy bears on their way to Heathrow Airport, London.

along with her other bear Mud, about ten years later, she was heartbroken. Patti still expects him to walk back into her life to this day.

As as result of this disappointment, Patti, together with Graham Cooke, decided to start the International Teddy Bear Club, to bring together like-minded people from all over the world, and put them in contact with each other. The Club has declared 1985 The Year of the Teddy Bear, and will be working with the Save the Children Fund, raising money for children all over the world to celebrate the United Nations Year of Youth. If you wish to join, write to the International Teddy Bear Club, 575 Madison Avenue, New York, New York 10022, enclosing $19.95 for your membership. The Club is open to people of all ages, and the oldest member is ninety! With your gold-embossed membership card, you get a fluffy little new bear with a round shiny nose, an enameled teddy bear button, and a packet containing a teddy bear book, a picture disk, with an authentic

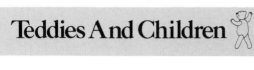

Left A British Brownie hugs her teddy bear at the Teddy Bear Rally at Longleat, England.

Below Baby twins strapped into their pushchair with their twin bears at Longleat.

early recording of the Teddy Bears' Picnic and a calendar. The Club will be producing a quarterly magazine, full of information, and addresses, plus two pages of Teddy Bear Pen Pals.

Children's Bears

There is obviously no need to throw away a bear if he gets a little worn. There are many expert people ready and willing to restore teddy, as far as possible, to his former glory. Nothing much can be done about balding plush, but many children (and adults) are proud of their hairless bears, and regard them as battle-scarred heroes. But leaking stuffing, loss of eyes and general collapse of the pads can be coped with at the following:

Elisabeth Edes, 8 Ridgeway East, Scarsdale, NY 10583.
Enchanted Valley Dolls' Hospital and Bear Refuge, 1700 McHenty Village Way, Apt 5, Modesto California.
The Dolls' Hospital, 787 Lexington Avenue, New York, NY 10021.
The Grizzlies, 223 W. Lloyd St, Pensacola, Florida 32501.
Anne Rees, 161 Primrose Way, Palo Alto, California 94303.
Dr S. Stern BD, Box 258-3, Sherwood, Oregon 97140.
Dr Lois Beck BD, 103000 Champaigne Lane, S.E. Portland, Oregon 97266.
Dr Dorothy Bordeaux, Rt 2, Box 760, Silver Springs, Florida.
Margaret Mett, 601 Taneytown Road, Gettysburg, Pennsylvania 17325.

Facing page, top Teddy bears picnicking.

Facing page. Big Ted, opposite below, who helps raise funds for Contact-a-Family, a British charity which brings together families with physically and mentally handicapped children to form neighborhood self-help groups, especially in isolated inner city and rural areas.

There is no need to tell you how special the teddy bear is. He has been around for over eighty years and has never slipped down the popularity stakes. Within five years of birth, almost every child in the United States had his or her own teddy to love. At first, he was seen as filling a need for a boys' toy, where girls had dolls. But boys and girls took to him equally, and maintained their affection well into adulthood. Many teddies have even been taken to the grave.

As Peter Bull said, "Childish? Teddy bears are no more childish than collecting wives, cars or yachts!"

Somewhere, a teddy bear sits quietly, waiting to be noticed, stretching out his arms and looking gently benevolent. Who could resist him?

Facing page and this page Some bears enjoying their day out at the Teddy Bears' Picnic at Longleat, in August 1982.

Facing page and this page In June 1982, London Zoo celebrated the centenary of A. A. Milne's birth with Bear Day at London Zoo. Christopher Robin called his famous teddy bear after his favorite zoo bear, Winnie, whom he used to feed with honey from a spoon. There were all sorts of different things to do: Lorne McKean, who sculpted the Winnie the Pooh statue at the Zoo was there with her husband to help children make statues of their own teddies. Enid Irving, who drew the pictures for Peter Bull's Bully Bear Books, was there with four other artists drawing portraits of teddy bears. Katy Stewart, who wrote the Winnie the Pooh cook book gave advice on cooking with honey. There were readings from Paddington's adventures and an exhibition of famous bears from London's Toy and Model Museum.

Children's pictures of their teddy bears, *left to right:* Peter, by Bryony Crompton aged 6; Teddy, by Jessica Henty, aged 4; Brown Teddy by Kate Ismay, aged 6; Parachuting Teddy, by Ben Shaw, aged 5; Burnt Teddy, by Heather Crompton, aged 8.

by
Heather

Above A goodnight kiss between a loving teddy bear and his child.

Left Chinese children in Peking with, appropriately enough, a Chinese panda bear.

Top Children become closely bound up with their teddies; they are quite ready to believe that teddies move when their back is turned.

Above Although teddy bears were originally thought of as boys' toys, little girls soon discover the joys of a furry friend, and some prefer teddies to hard cold dolls.

Right Teddies play a vital role in hospital – if a child sees his teddy receiving treatment bravely, he will far more readily submit and feel much more confident.

Top and bottom right For many children, it would be impossible to go to sleep without their teddy to comfort them in the dark.

Above Shirley Temple and a huge teddy bearing birthday greetings on one of Rose Wharnsby's fascinating old postcards.

Facing page A very small girl with a very large teddy, at Longleat.

Above Teddy bears add an extra dimension to the lives of all their admirers. They have done nothing but good throughout the 83 years of their existence.

Left Teddy bears of the four main kinds: panda bear, koala bear, polar bear and brown bear. The little creatures are now inseparable from us: fads may come and go, but teddy bear will be around for ever.

PICTURE CREDITS

Aldus Archive 21 **Allsport** 10, 11 bottom **Alresford Crafts Limited** 63 bottom **Hanna Barbara** 37 right **Canterbury Bears** 50, 51 top, 51 bottom **Stephanie Colasanti** 90-91 **Contact a Family** 82 bottom **Forest Service U.S.D.A.** 14 right **French Wools** 70 **Granada Television** 35 left **Tim Graham** 43 top **Ronald Grant Archive** 39 top **House of Nisbet** 53 top **Image Bank** David W Hamilton 64 bottom **Chris Turner** 63 top **International Teddy Bear Club** 16-17 **Enid Irving** 9 bottom, 31 bottom, 35 right, 40-41 **Camilla Jessel** 92 bottom **Patrick Matthews** 36, 37 top left, 37 bottom left **Methuen Children's Books Limited** 14 left, 18 **Penny Millar** 95 top **Multimedia Publications (UK) Limited** Jon Bouchier contents, 6-7, 15 top left, 15 bottom left, 24 bottom right, 27 bottom, 28, 29 bottom right, 42 bottom, 44-45, 46 top, 48 left, 49 top right, 52 top left, 53 bottom left, 53 bottom right, 56, 57 top right, 58, 59, 60-61, 62 left, 62 bottom, 64 top left, 64 bottom, 65 bottom, 66-67, 68 top, 68 bottom, 69 bottom, 96, endpapers **Philip de Bay** 22 **Geoff Howard** 52 top right, 52 bottom right, 52 bottom left, 78-79 **Paul Jenkins** 20, 25 **Peter Newark's Western Americana** 9 top **Richard Olivier** half title 43 bottom, 76-77, 83 top, 84, 85 **Petit Format** Claire de Virieu 91, 92 top **Sandra Lousada** 94, 92 left **Photographers' Library** 27 top, 57 top, 62 left, 64 top right, 65 top, 69 top **PictureBank Photo Library** 12 top, 93 top, 93 bottom right **Picture Search/Neill Meneer** 30 bottom **Popperfoto** 8 bottom **Rex Features** 26 top, 38, 42 top, 81 bottom, 82 top **John Rigby** 34 top, 34 bottom, 40 left, 46 bottom, 47 top, 47 bottom **Simplicity Patterns** 95 bottom **Siriol Animation Limited** 31 top **Sotheby's London** 11 top, 12, 13, 48 right, 55 **Spectrum** 8 top **Superted Distributions Limited** 30 top **Topham** 23, 24 top, 24 bottom left, 39 bottom **Vogue** title **Vogue Pattern Service** 74-75 **Patrick Ward** 32, 80, 81 top, 86 top, 86 bottom, 87 **The Wareham Bears/Acorn Press** 54 top, 54 bottom **Rose Wharmsby** 15 right, 49 top left, 49 bottom, 57 bottom, 93 left

14 left and 18-19 Line illustrations by Ernest H Shepard Copyright under the Berne Convention. Copyright in the United States 1926 by E P Dutton & Co. Inc. Copyright renewal 1954 by A A Milne. Coloring of the illustration copyright © 1973 by Ernest H. Shepard and Methuen Children's Books Ltd. Reproduced by Permission of Curtis Brown Limited, London

22 Pencil sketch for Winnie the Pooh Copyright © 1985 by Lloyds Bank Ltd and Colin Anthony Richards, Executors of the Estate of E H Shepard and the E H Shepard Trust. Reproduced by Permission of Curtis Brown Limited, London. Collection Victoria and Albert Museum, London

26 bottom © Illustration Peggy Fortnum and William Collins, Sons & Co., Ltd, 1983. From the **Paddington Story Book**, Published by Collins, 1983

29 top © Illustration by Willy Shermelé, **Fireside Tales**, Purnell Books, 1979

29 bottom left © Express Newspapers

24 bottom right, 27 bottom, 29 bottom right, 48 left, 53 bottom left, 57 top, 64 top, 64 bottom, 65 and endpapers were photographed at Hamley's Regent Street, London

Multimedia Books Limited have endeavoured to observe the legal requirements with regard to the suppliers of photographic material.

96